REFUGEE

For Jamie —

I'm so glad we discovered
your poetry last year. May
all refugees find home... that
includes birds!

With love and
respect,

Pam Uschuk

REFUGEE

∾

poems

~~Pamela Uschuk~~

Pamela Uschuk [signature]

🐓 Red Hen Press | *Pasadena, CA*

Book design by Mark E. Cull

Library of Congress Cataloging-in-Publication Data

Names: Uschuk, Pamela, author.
Title: Refugee : poems / Pamela Uschuk.
Description: First Edition. | Pasadena, CA : Red Hen Press, [2022] |
    Includes bibliographical references.
Identifiers: LCCN 2021031841 (print) | LCCN 2021031842 (ebook) | ISBN
    9781636280196 (trade paperback) | ISBN 9781636280202 (epub)
Subjects: LCGFT: Poetry.
Classification: LCC PS3571.S38 R44 2022 (print) | LCC PS3571.S38 (ebook)
    | DDC 811/.54—dc23
LC record available at https://lccn.loc.gov/2021031841
LC ebook record available at https://lccn.loc.gov/2021031842

The National Endowment for the Arts, the Los Angeles County Arts Commission,
the Ahmanson Foundation, the Dwight Stuart Youth Fund, the Max Factor Family
Foundation, the Pasadena Tournament of Roses Foundation, the Pasadena Arts &
Culture Commission and the City of Pasadena Cultural Affairs Division, the City of
Los Angeles Department of Cultural Affairs, the Audrey & Sydney Irmas Charitable
Foundation, the Kinder Morgan Foundation, the Meta & George Rosenberg Foundation,
the Albert and Elaine Borchard Foundation, the Adams Family Foundation, the
Riordan Foundation, Amazon Literary Partnership, the Sam Francis Foundation, and
the Mara W. Breech Foundation partially support Red Hen Press.

First Edition
Published by Red Hen Press
www.redhen.org

ACKNOWLEDGMENTS

ANTHOLOGIES:
Academy of American Poets, "Poem-A-Day," chosen by Poet Laureate Joy Harjo for 2020 National Poetry Month: "Green Flame"; *Coffee Poems Anthology*, ed. Lorraine Healy (World Enough Writers 2019): "Morning Coffee"; *Continental Drift*, ed. Drucilla Wall (University of Nebraska Press 2017): "With a Hurricane, She Climbs Mountains while She Dreams"; *The Heart's Many Doors: American Poets Respond to Metka Krašovec's Images Responding to Emily Dickinson*, ed. Richard Jackson (Wings Press 2017): "Inter-Peritoneal Chemo," "Levitation," and "Skull Song"; and *What Saves Us: Poems of Empathy and Outrage in the Age of Trump*, ed. Martín Espada (Northwestern University Press 2019): "A History of Morning Clouds and Contrails" and "Cracking 100."

JOURNALS:
About Place Blog, "Writing the Pandemic": "No April Fools"; *About Place Journal: Roots + Resistance*: "Let Them Eat Cake"; *About Place Journal: The Future Imagined Differently*: "Spring Runoff"; *Aeolian Harp*, vol. 4: "Endangered Species," "On Losing a Mother," "Shapeshifter," "Song of Reprieve," and "Toward Wings"; *Aeolian Harp*, vol. 6: "One to Count Cadence"; *Blue Heron Review*: "Axis" and "Dog Walk Song"; *Clade Song*, #8: "Good Friday at Old Pascua"; *Dove Tales*: "Refuge"; *Gamut*: "Bulk"; *Gargoyle*: "Aggravated Child Theft" and "Speaking of Angels and Ghosts"; *Ghost Town*: "Contemplating Fire on a Spring Desert Evening," "Desert Aubade," and "Finding a Moth Dead on the Windowsill"; *New World Writing*: "Fox Sighting in Phoenix," "Healing Song for Surgery," "Solar Eclipse in the Land of Sandstone Hoodoos and Cranes," "Voyager," and "Walking the Labyrinth"; *Passages North*: "A History of Morning Clouds And Contrails"; *Pirene's Fountain: Skin Deep*: "Dharma"; *Pirene's Fountain: Tenth Anniversary Issue*: "Holograms"; *Poems & Plays*: "Giving Up"; *Poetry Miscellany*: "Stormlight"; *Terrain.org, Dear America* series: "After the Election, a Super Moon Rises Over the Rincon Mountains"; *Three Coyotes Review*: "Phoebe"; *Texas Poetry Calendar*: "The Morning Porch"; and *Vox Populi*: "Bordering on Hysteria," "Cracking 100," and "Refuge."

BROADSIDES:
The Max Papers: "Morning Coffee" and "Talking Crow." PEN INTERNATIONAL WOMEN (especially Judyth Hill) featured me reading poems, from this ms., "Cracking 100," "Green Flame," and "Aggravated Child Theft" from this ms. in two International human rights readings in 2020.

This collection of poems is dedicated to Val Uschuk,
Terry Acevedo, and Lynn Watt
who inspire me with their courage, senses of humor, and creativity
to help me thrive with grace
and dedicated with love to my partner-in-love, William Pitt Root,
and his daughter Jennifer Lorca Root—
my heart family I could not do without

I also want to thank friends who've read and made suggestions for poems in this book and those whose caring friendship has been a great support—Fenton Johnson, Olivia Garza, Joy Harjo, Teri Hairston, Linda Hogan, Cynthia Hogue, Patricia Jabbeh Wesley, Melissa Pritchard, Melissa Studdard, Marilyn Kallet, Terri Harvey, Richard Jackson, Carmen Calatayud, Peggy Shumaker, Donley Watt, Kate Bell, Lucy Clark, Luis Alberto Urrea, Pat Campeau, Jesse Tsinajinnie Maloney, Lindsay Royce, Patricia Spears Jones, Ron Fundingsland, and Michael McDermott. Deep gratitude to my students and colleagues who are more valuable than diamonds. I appreciate my nieces, Julia Brooks and Emilie Rose Cranson, as well as nephews, Lyndy, Maxwell, Sam, Seth, and Pat, who enrich my life for being most themselves.

And for those dear relatives who have passed from this earth—my sister Judi Uschuk-Stahl, Aunt Olga, Bud Uschuk, George Moberg, Jim Sleight, and my brother, John Uschuk.

Thank you Michael McDermott and the Black Earth Institute for choosing me as a fellow for 2018–2022. This institute is devoted to addressing social issues through the arts, science, and spirituality, and has widened and wisened my view as well as has given me new and brilliant friends.

And an abundance of love to Zazu, my rescue dog, Mojo Buffalo Buddy, and Sadie Cat.

Most of all, thank you to Kate Gale and Red Hen Press for accepting and believing in this book, and thank you to Natasha McClellan and Rebeccah Sanhueza for shepherding me through the process!

CONTENTS

SKULL SONG

    A History of Morning Clouds and Contrails   15

    Bulk   17

    With a Hurricane, She Climbs

        Mountains While She Dreams   20

    Cracking One Hundred   22

    Aggravated Child Theft   23

    Skull Song   24

    Bass Note   25

AXIS

    Spring Runoff   29

    Dog Walk Song   30

    Axis   31

    Beyond Oxygen   33

    Giving Up   36

    Barred Owl at Equinox   39

    Phoebe   41

    Talking Crow   42

    Stormlight   43

    Fox Sighting in Phoenix   44

    Endangered Species   45

LIQUID BOOK OF THE DEAD

Healing Song for Surgery   51

Pathology Report   52

Shapeshifter   53

Intraperitoneal Chemo   54

Green Flame   55

Toward Wings   56

Song of Reprieve   57

On Losing a Mother   58

Dharma   60

Walking the Labyrinth   61

Theories of Time   65

Olivia Begins Chemotherapy   67

Solar Eclipse in the Land of

     Sandstone Hoodoos and Cranes   69

Finding a Moth Dead on the Windowsill   70

Singing Bowl   71

SPEAKING OF ANGELS AND GHOSTS

Western Tanager   75

Morning Coffee   77

Weather Change   78

Refuge   80

Bordering on Hysteria   82

Web   84

The Morning Porch   85

Speaking of Angels and Ghosts   87

One to Count Cadence   89

Holograms   90

After the Election, the Super Moon Rises

     Over the Rincon Mountains   91

Let Them Eat Cake   93

Good Friday at Old Pascua   95

Contemplating Fire on a Spring Desert Evening   96

No April Fools   97

Levitation   98

Desert Aubade   99

The Essential Shape   100

Gardenias at Easter   102

My silences had not protected me. Your silence will not protect you. But for every real word spoken, for every attempt I had ever made to speak those truths for which I am still seeking, I had made contact with other women while we examined the words to fit a world in which we all believed, bridging our differences.

—Audre Lorde, *The Cancer Journals*

Try to praise the mutilated world.
Remember June's long days,
and wild strawberries, drops of wine, the dew.
The nettles that methodically overgrow
the abandoned homesteads of exiles.
You must praise the mutilated world.
You watched the stylish yachts and ships;
one of them had a long trip ahead of it,
while salty oblivion awaited others.
You've seen the refugees heading nowhere,
you've heard the executioners sing joyfully.
You should praise the mutilated world.
Remember the moments when we were together
in a white room and the curtain fluttered.
Return in thought to the concert where music flared.
You gathered acorns in the park in autumn
and leaves eddied over the earth's scars.
Praise the mutilated world
and the grey feather a thrush lost,
and the gentle light that strays and vanishes
and returns.

—Adam Zagajewski, *Try to Praise the Mutilated World*

SKULL SONG

A HISTORY OF MORNING CLOUDS AND CONTRAILS

So you think that you can live remote
from city streets paved with bullet casings,
mass shootings in churches, refugee mothers in cages,
the beheadings of girls sprayed from cable TV.

While the intricate lace burka of contrails smothers dawn's blush,
sky blasts dogma to smithereens over mountains
too distant to notice the woman barricaded
down the road at Fox Fire,
her automatic rifle aimed at police.

Each morning, ravens carve black questions
that go unanswered by light. Assailed
by headwinds, they sheer, intent on laughter
as they bank nearly upside down to sing.

Sun climbs hand over burning hand
through aspen leaves going to gold bullion
anyone can spend regardless
of what bank they believe in.

Go out, lie in last season's sinking tomato bed, pull
dead plants around you and spit seeds
at the chemical ooze of contrails jets expel
bisecting the blue intelligence of sky's water dreams,
crosshatching quadrants between clouds
gauzy as love slipping between finger cracks.

The woman is desperate, mistakes bullets
she jams in her ex-husband's gun for

her own screams, for his incessant fists.
How else can she feel safe? She, too,
inhales toxins saturating sky.

Feel the warmth of an otter's last dive
before ice takes the river. Police sirens
fade like contrails across the exhausted heart of this land.
What we relinquish in the name of security
manipulates what we would breathe.

BULK

Running on the treadmill, I am thinking about bulk,
the bulk of an elephant blocking sun
as she walks past, baby
grasping her tail, letting go,
the tarpaulin bulk of her ears flapping at flies, goodbyes
trumpeting from her trunk
tender enough to sense a bruise
on her baby's ankle, trunk
that can wrap a banyan tree
uprooting it for lunch.

Consider the bulk of a manatee,
as big as a taxi, nearly weightless
in the clear blue eye of a limestone springs,
manatee, levitating toward the bulk
of my brother, lips touching his diving mask,
tenderness he missed in his youth.

I am thinking about bulk,
the bulk of a propeller as it slices
through calm waterways,
bulk of water lilies manatee eats
with flippers bigger than my head,
manatee's utterly harmless bulk
gouged by the propeller's whirl.

Or dark bulk, the sheer weight of bandoliers,
lines of bullets fed into a machine gun,
the weight of an Israeli Humvee wracking Gaza streets,
missiles and bombs vaporizing mothers,

children at play in streets, the weight of the Torah,
Koran, King James Bible,
a mosque door made of myrtle, its
perfumed density, bulk of marble and powdered ruby
illuminating the Taj Mahal by full moonlight.

I am thinking about bulk, my brother's six-foot, three-inch
bulk, his large hands stroking the manatee's face, both
of them weighing less in water than a bale of straw,
squinting at one another, their graceful
balancing, lithe as clouds.

I am thinking about bulk, the
small bulk of a seven-year-old refugee
detained and dying of dehydration
and high fever on a border patrol bus, the bulk
of the mistake, lead tears
annealing the world.

I am thinking about bulk
and the female elephant
and the weight of tusks
and the African sun branding everything.

There is the bulk of one thousand pounds of elephant
fed daily to troops slaughtered by wildlife guards
because of a lack of beef. Within
a decade this bulk will cease to be.

The weight of guilt passes from husband
to wife, father to son to son to son, a feather
of guilt that stops all flight.

I am thinking about bulk,
the bulk of flowers, say gardenias
or tuber roses or lilacs in the spring,
the weight of perfume, funereal,
lotus blossoms manatee hugs to her chest to eat.

WITH A HURRICANE, SHE CLIMBS
MOUNTAINS WHILE SHE DREAMS

When she leans against aspen trunks,
she hears ice storms roar through
the gold coinage of leaves, a rush
like wind under the ocean, rattle
of blood in veins as big as her arms.

Above ten thousand feet, bark toddler skin smooth, folded
and elephantine, fits to her ear
like a cool herbal sachet.

Clarified by the wildfire of early fall leaves, sun dogs
leap from peak to high peak, transparent
as stained glass, bioluminescent as breath
passing up through the woody heart.

Rain soaks her dreams of flight, nails all night
wet hawk primaries to their dusky roosts
while Congress debates our skewed history of torture techniques—
which raw beatings to lose, which waterboarding to keep.

All night, her rescue dog snuggles close her thigh.
Lightning spikes thunder's huge and terrible mouth
until dawn ravens croak through cloud rags, what
is left of the hurricane from the invisible gulf.

She holds silver sunrise, wafer of searing hope
under her tongue. Ice rain slicks
the bark of aspens in their distant nurseries,

far from feverish mothers barb-wired
in detention camps in Nogales, milk
crusting their blouse fronts, away from
their children, caged, curled into question marks
on military foil blankets scarring the news.

CRACKING ONE HUNDRED

for Terry Acevedo

Near the border, preschoolers worry about butterflies.
How can they fly over the wall? Twenty-foot-tall, thick steel plates
would sear delicate wings. And, lizards, Miss,
how can they get through?
Small fingers draw orange wings crashing into steel,
lizards hanging their blue heads. *Y el tigre?*
Severing ancient migration paths, the wall
will ensure the jaguar's end.

Just after *Cinco de Mayo*, daytime temps
crack the knuckles of one hundred, ten degrees above normal.
No wall can stop rising heat, the death of coral reefs
or the governor calling for the National Guard to secure the border.
In holding cells, children separated from deported parents
wait for a future no one can predict.
And, in the San Joaquin Valley, strawberries and tomatoes
rot in fields. Farmers wonder where the pickers have gone.

Immaculate in his Armani suit, the President tweets
for congressional support to build his wall, calls for
a prayer meeting in the Oval Office. You can hear
Bible hymns hum behind bulletproof doors
across the lush White House lawn where Monarch butterflies,
who've migrated all the way from Mexico, land
on bright rose petals tended by hands
the same color as earth that nourishes them.

AGGRAVATED CHILD THEFT

On Gibraltar, a male macaque swipes a baby to gift an enemy
who's defeated him, baring teeth in a bizarre smile,
while the alpha victor turns the infant screeching
upside down, sniffs the terrorized bottom until
both males grin, the fuse of enmity snuffed.
Hours later, the traumatized baby is returned.

Because "everyone" wants him to win the Nobel Peace Prize,
our president decrees children of Central American immigrants
be separated from parents, caged until placed
in foster homes, child theft on a grand old party scale,
criminal deterrent to illegal crossings.

Remember Terezín? Children torn from Jewish mothers
herded on trains to be gassed in Treblinka, Dachau?
The orphans at Terezín (Heaven in German), fattened
up, until a propaganda film for the model camp could be shot.

Far from the Statue of Liberty, ICE confiscates
thousands of toddlers and children wrenched screaming from
the arms of mothers seeking asylum, our history of shame
hooked on the coiled razor-wire laws of inhumanity.
Unlike macaque babies, kidnapped refugees will not be returned.

SKULL SONG

> *I've seen a Dying Eye*
> *Run round and round a room.*
> —Emily Dickinson

How often the skull charred at the sockets turns
to watch the heart. It's an old story. Old as rabbit
jittered, kicking gravel at coyote's jaws ready
to snap the sweet spot at the back of his neck.

In the rock grotto above San Xavier Mission, a daughter
tosses the dark braid of her mother, charred at one end
to the feet of the Virgin of Guadalupe
whose eyes are on heaven and its endless grief.

Rabbit and coyote have been in love for years, often watch
the icy eye of Venus die at dawn, while all the white-winged doves
in the city line up on electric wires, thrumming up sun
before hawk takes sky's skull almost tenderly in its skree.

BASS NOTE

for Teri Hairston and Dorianne Laux

How does the pen levitate
        as it contemplates the sorrow
of the extra bass string
                on a violin
crafted to carry grief. The city smokes
        beyond the poet's fingertips
that would learn an underpass past loss, the way
                graffiti is a kind of music, strident
concert spraying need on bridges,
                        on sealed
box cars carrying deceptive toys stained
with toxic paint.

                        This improvised canvas riffs
        jazz notes flying from a pen
saxophone or bass guitar
                any poet can pick up,
                                play
snapping vulture-necked betrayal,
        breaking
heartbreak's borders
dividing this charcoal metroscape.

AXIS

SPRING RUNOFF

Nameless tiny lilac flowers sing wanton as finches
cosseted by grass near Los Pinos River
tumescent with runoff the color of cappuccino on a humid day in Venice
when love was a hand full of violets lusting
in a foreign tongue thrust down my throat.
I refuse to gather these perfect purple blooms, knowing
they live longer in their own thawed soil,
along this water rushing wild as sex in another life.

DOG WALK SONG

for Billy Root

Past young aspen and punky old balsa alike,
before sunrise unhinges lids from speech,
the boy in him walks the dogs to the river,
the best part of his day, he says, autumn river
swiveling to grind the stones of his imagination,
carrying ice from the spring that cracks granite
at thirteen thousand feet, where forget-me-nots
blood-drop small breed late, where
          eagle feeds on voles, and
a bull elk swells his thick neck bugling to mate.
Above him, magpies rock the pear tree
shading the grave of the wolf
who lopes underground now, grave
of his wild white heart gone to the stars.
The boy in him laughs at the new pup
shaped like something between a black bear
and a buffalo stumbling and biting through his own leash.

The boy in him has given up on restraints, mind
careening free as the torrent pouring over boulders,
cutting through the park named after eagles
who will return with first snow.
The boy in him walks the dogs to this river
he kayaks to his further life carved
          from wolf willows of hope
bent by storm and offering themselves supple
to wind's knife whittling hawk song,
late wild bloom, shadow-swell,
deer-licked dawn.

AXIS

I

Rain-slick in the lower pasture, two new foals
fall like wet garbage bags from their mothers, flatten
onto grass.
           The mare bites through the birth sac, and
the colt shakes up on splayed knees,
                     breathes.

Before noon, the universe is his.
He gallops circles around his dam, neat
stallion hooves flicking skyward. Oh,
to be alive. Jive joyful. Migrating
      vultures turn sky's invisible axis
              over his twin sister, who still cannot rise.

II

I read tea leaves. Love smears the rim, where
memory floats me in a kayak on the Sea of Cortez, amazed
at the glassy swell of water lifting
above gorse weed and coral
and the one red reef fish
hovering in an oar's shadow, pretending to pray.

Perched atop lava rock, blue-footed boobies
and pelicans preened, lifting to scatter
when some internal radar screen
alerted them to a school of yellow tails
hidden beneath the rough thrust of waves.
I wish I was that untroubled, not adrift

and paddling against undertow current
with nowhere to go
while my husband threw sticks for dogs running the beach.

Watching dolphins breach off Soledad Estuario,
we stumbled on what wind dredged—
a bleached and rotting moray eel, and
the dolphin, strangled by a gill net, cinched
and bloated into two blotchy pink sacks
split like our hearts at the seams.

III

Now, Brewer's blackbirds wade for bugs
through an ocean of thick green.
Do they hear horses stampede through
the muddy fields of my heart, locked
in spring snow that refuses all attempts to melt?

On crooked legs, the twin suckles.
Eyeing the steady cyclone of vultures above
her brother cranes his beautiful new neck.
This time, the filly survives. I pull my jacket tight,
missing eagles who've flown to the high country,
whose wings all winter were the one certainty
giving cadence to the disassembling air.

BEYOND OXYGEN

Cheval, caballo, loshad, horse, each
muscle bunched, a boulder
of power moving beneath sunhot skin.

Horse sees
the world nearly 360 degrees
through the largest eyes of any land mammal,
holds the history of love
and wounds
in her wide sight,
piercing our cerebral fear.

At full gallop, horse breathes shallow, the only
being who can run beyond oxygen,
miles before dropping of a burst heart.
Horse completes any landscape, tossing
beauty to the sky, mane and lush tail
tangling wild as she four steps
a waltz around her rearing mate.

Give me the huff of a thoroughbred, black
legs pumping through loose sod, hackles
collapsing the far track's curve, ears
tucked back to her own lunging heartbeat,
dawn fog
smelling of clover and sawdust, the steady chuff
of thunder hooves thudding into earth's flesh
the sexual joy of speed, flexed shoulders
and thighs gleaming sweat, sweat,

sweat, to please
the slight-boned rider clamped to her back.

Or a mustang galloping over lupine to a sandstone ridge
where he bucks, kicks thin air,
jerks his head clear of biting flies, the echo
of his stampede beating bedrock
and dust lodging in his heaving lungs,
unsaddled by his lust.
He leads

his harem along cliff's edge, past
a cougar den to sweet grass lining a creek.

Alone in high country after my sister died,
no longer able to breathe,
I stood at an unraveling barbwire fence
and watched a herd of quarter horses race straight at me,
eight horses outweighing me by thousands of pounds.

I did not leap away or scream. *Go ahead,*
I said.

Their hooves, that could easily have split my ribcage
and skull, stopped inches away.
Stretching their necks, the mares
read me with nostrils soft as Chinese silk.

Feeding them grass, I scratched
the long bones of their faces

leaning into my own.
       Even the yearlings were careful not to bruise
my sandaled feet. Their unbearable
          gentle muzzles broke
through the ulcerated curtain of long grief.

We'd known each other all our years.
Shooing flies from their eyes, I whispered
prayers in satin ears flicking against my cheeks,
knew then gratitude with no expectation, love
pungent as rain
          rivering gigantic flanks
that turned and sauntered into dusk dissolving the trees.

GIVING UP

for Darlin Neal and Elayne Silversmith

I

Florida photo trip. We rent kayaks
to frame the perfect shot of manatees
and roseate spoonbills, lacey egrets,
yellow-beaked night herons alert for gators
as they fish tea-colored shallows
shifting the mangrove swamp.

Decades we've searched for them, bought
stuffed manatee beanies for nieces,
multiple pairs of dugong earrings, pasted
Save The Manatee bumper stickers
on cars from Colorado to New York and back,
hired guides in Florida and Mexico, baffled
by the singularity of their failure to appear.
Lonely weeks I sat on hope's Gulf coast dock
where daily before his death, they'd shown up for my brother.

Paddling into stiff sea wind, I recall the Himalayas, how
each day I searched for what sherpas promised
looked like a bush tumbling diagonal across a slope,
the sky-eyed snow leopard
loping spectral on paws the size of my head.
Squinting through binoculars, I spotted
treeless skree, the fiery shimmie of icemelt,
an occasional yak and Pashmina sheep, heard
the thick screams of Himalayan eagles diving
through dizzy ozone, but never those
sacred winter-colored roars, wild sutras I longed for.

II

Nothing is accidental. Elayne found a mule deer fawn,
newborn, atop the mountain pass,
its mother smashed by a pickup's grille.
She scooped up the fawn the way her Diné grandmother
lifted baby goats, cradling it to her kitchen,
taught the newborn to suck from a human bottle
before she released it to rehabilitators near the Rez.

Next week Elayne leaves to be the new librarian
at the Smithsonian in DC, the fawn rescue
the blessing she packs against urban eastern wind.

III

Around bend after leaf-spackled bend, snow-bright
egrets transmogrify shade, proving
again mystery beats manifest belief.
Tired, we paddle into the roiled cove
where we see huge bodies
gray as marl studded by hair plugs, giants
slamming tails and hurling
whale-sized chests atop one another,
drenching us and muddying the lagoon.
Our guide hisses, "Stay back, away
from them. Manatees," he laughs, "are clumsy
when, um, distracted by sex."

Into the beautiful welter, I guide my kayak
as my husband clicks shot after shot.
I fail to see the female who dives below me
until the heave.
                    I freeze,
when, as gentle as a priestess offering incense to sky,
                she lifts and I am
        weightless as birdsong in a tangle of seagrass,
sharing the stunned light mermaids breathe.

BARRED OWL AT EQUINOX

for Marilyn Kallet

Grandma Anna taught me not to listen to owl hoots,
to avoid their daylight stares.
So today, I nearly miss the barred owl,
dumpy, unkempt, squatting
camouflaged between two white oaks, focused
on what we fear—
a fat water moccasin the color of wet mud
coiled on a rotting log in black backwater,
where peepers *treep treep treep*
sharp as the pileated woodpecker's rap
sounding hollow wood.

Each time owl shuffle-hops to another limb,
squirrel flicks his tail's come-eat-me tease.
      We eco poets thrill
          to watch his rarity
hunker into thick brown down hiding his death intent.

          Squirrel is wired as a terrier, snapped
synapses rattling a few feet from talons.
    This cheeky teen has no fear, dis-throws
insults at a puffed-up tyrant, risking everything.

Despite binoculars, a spotting scope
that can nail a mole on a child's hand, we lose
him in the suffocating twist of Southern leaves.
When he flies from his perch, we die a little,
awed by the soundless sough
of his huge wings, deft even as they tilt
through the swamp's impossible mesh.

In one talon thrust, owl impales
a yard long garter snake
as if to say,

I take the feast I need.
What about you?

He knows he owns us, flaunts the snake
whipping between limbs back to the oak to eat.

With one nip of his yellow beak, he quick
snips off the head, sips
the entire reptile like limp linguine.
Drunk on his meal, owl stares beyond
our scrawled field notes.

For decades, I have sought out rare wings,
memorized songs to remember my own.
What composes owl's bass line
echoing my deepest childhood fear?

At our feet, nations of petals—trout lilies,
celanian poppies, lobed toothworts, trillium
slender as lemon flames.
It's Equinox and we consider balance
While lightning bugs turn leaves to constellations,
an eagle circles above owl, above us
and the canopy of moonless night. Opens.

PHOEBE

The phoebe whistles its two-syllable name
through rain that's hung itself overnight
in stormstruck trees. Rain tips
blooms so small I have to kneel to identify them—
Johnny jump-ups, bluettes, blood-colored buds,
unlike yellow jasmine, forsythia blasting
open hedgerows, rioting in the streets.

I worship their muddy feet. Woven through sod
buttery tongues tiny enough to be inlaid in my fingernails are
an incantation to mercy's kingdom
against jets strafing Syrian crowds,
the radiation-sizzled skin of children
stretched to tragic pixels on a TV screen.

News analysts shift facts while the human world rocks
sobbing in its bandages of betrayal,
ears seared deep by lies.
Here in Appalachian foothills, calm petals
surround the corpse of the huge old oak
downed by night's microburst, blaze
sudden as plutonium from a crack in evitable clouds.

Knoxville, Tennessee

TALKING CROW

for Teri Hairston

From the live oak, crows pull dead leaves,
spearing them with crow black beaks.
Day dries folded wings over the Carolinas where
sky weeps pavement a darker shade of tears.
Here bullet holes chip downtown streets,
alternative facts to ropes slung over oak
branches that still remember each broken neck,
dangling pairs of feet, blues sung in the key of fear.
Don't shoot. Don't
shoot
Don't shoot folds into the vocal cords of mothers, wives,
streaming down a child's witness face
crows, quick to imitate, learn.

Winston-Salem, North Carolina

STORMLIGHT

for Richard Jackson

The Tennessee River runs murky as yesterday's coffee, slops
over ruined banks, bubbles through drowned
muskrat holes, muddying the meditations of grass.
Gone are tumescent gray thunderheads, funnel
winds husking farms, freight cars, gone
the viridian roar ripping roofs from classrooms, homes,
malls, splitting metal sheets as easy as tender skin.
Mobile homes don't stand a chance, blown
apart like boxes of potato chips, smashing
kids and single moms who still owe on them.
Sky's deceptive smile does not mourn their deaths.
Across swollen current the spring woods
are soft as a Turner landscape, light
as definite as the facets of a cut crystal bowl, trees
harmless as broccoli rooted in limestone.
Over the flood, blue heron wings unhinge
to find new roots. You'd never guess
how sky shimmied as wild and green
as love's unappeased ache, that
sixty tornadoes sliced havoc's swath
through the vulnerable bones of half a dozen states.
Megastorms, weathermen say, are the new norm.
Micro-bursts gust to splinter old-growth oaks.
Get used to torrential rains, hail the size of grapefruit
that blasts windshields, bashes double-pane glass.
Climate change is unpopular but real.
What survives is a cardinal's tenor sax note
stunning a sweet gum tree, buttercups
bending to wind's raw moods,
Musk-trumpeting honeysuckle vine tangles
strict afterstorm light, strangling new leaves.

FOX SIGHTING IN PHOENIX

Sometimes a fox can scar our lives, opening
us with eyes firefly green, two sizzling moons
bioluminescent at murky midnight.

After chemo, we see her slim body, a silent negative blur
as gray as an x-ray of an abdomen diseased,
elusive as a suture completely healed.

Siren regarding us, she stands on the roof,
warns us against the spinning wheel of meaning and deceit,
the coming of enemies we will need to forgive.

We reach out to ancestors pillaging dreams
to deliver messages we strain to interpret.
From the eave, fox leaps soundless to solid ground.

The path through the labyrinth is forgiveness.
Each pain is a sword hacking open the self
congealed on desire fed by narcissist fire.

Fox shows herself only by moonlight.
Survivor of rush hour traffic and cement block walls,
she leaves her secret warren, her kits deep in the city's whirred gut.

We watch the grease of her glide
substantiating the dark before she disappears,
her eyes twin novas in shadows she eats.

ENDANGERED SPECIES

for Judi-Uschuk-Stahl, 1953–2015

In Costa Rica, our guide, a muralist, says
the red-backed squirrel monkey is extinct
in the park, the one monkey I'd flown thousands
of miles for, its creamy face sweet as white chocolate
after summer's diet of chewing bitter leaves.

This thatched canopy of figs and marvelous trees
hosts thousands of diverse bromeliads
and vines, trees dripping color like smooth elephant legs
that have been dipped in tie-dyed neon.

Done whoop-roaring by 9:00 a.m., howler monkeys
drape arms and legs over high limbs to snooze
having chewed too many hallucinogens.
In altered states above the commerce of our lives,
they'll dream away the heated day.

At the beach, Capuchins squat on lithe black legs
scouting treats in sweaty tourist hands.
Their alabaster faces are wise in the ways of theft
and self-sustainability. Deft, a monkey swoops
to snatch a teen's bag of chips
with fingertips as delicate as breath.

My sister would have liked it here close to the Equator,
throwing back her mahogany hair, thrilled
as I by the bright red and black Halloween crabs
big as my face crawling the rainforest floor
or by the black hawk hanging drenched wings
over its leaf-lit perch. I hear her fountain laugh,

the way she chuckled at me where two contrails
crossed a sundog just a week after her death, saying
"From this great distance, everything looks
funny down there." Released from her wheelchair,
she ran through thunderheads to stop my tears.

When Roy shakes his head at the disappearance
of squirrel monkeys from the medicine world, I think
how we are all endangered. It's not been a month since
my sister vanished taking her unblemished skin,
her beautiful sarcasm and last dusky breath.
Not one of us expected her to die. I can hardly bear
the sultry sun, the stun of blue ocean or the sweet child
trying to feed that Capuchin a piece of his banana.

Back at the hotel, I snap photos of blue trumpet flowers.
Their petals widen for attention.
I frame Roy's mural, a mélange of scarlet macaws
bloodying sky above the trees, a three-toed sloth with Li Po's face,
and, above Roy's signature, a red-backed squirrel monkey
staring for eternity at a chlorinated swimming pool.

What looks like a small bag of groceries
tumbles through banana leaves past my head.
I cringe, squint at the unbelievable neon fur
orange as a courtesan's skirt, the creamy furred face
questioning mine. Granting my last wish,
the monkey lets me see his body full view
making Roy's painting come true.

What had been extinct is close as my hand,

mumbling at me in the language of memory and time.

We stare at one another. My husband's camera clicks.

This extinction poses for shot after shot.

I can almost touch his fiery mantle,

his lost vitality resurrected

in a jungle tangled with endangered leaves.

LIQUID BOOK OF THE DEAD

HEALING SONG FOR SURGERY

for Happy

White wolf of healing, howl bone long
through the surgeon's poised hands. Steady
any tremor, correct errors,
torque dreams gone wrong,
rendering them to broth
numinous as the blade that incises skin
shaped by generations of guard hairs,
dens squirming with pups left to a wolf uncle's tender nips,
centuries of loping blue through snow drifts
guided by the wheel of constellations in your yellow eyes.

White wolf of healing, lap milk from moon shadows,
lope away from disease, from malfunction
to the center of the immutable,
sliced by fine tempered steel.

PATHOLOGY REPORT

after Ovarian Cancer Surgery

Bruised jaundice, dawn's wound leaks blood.
Day's scalpel slices to widen the gap for hysterectomy,
to remove all hysterical desire, flesh and mind
anesthetized, numb as a tomb.
Vacuum tumors, uterus, ovaries, fallopian tubes,
omentum's entire gelatinous shield.
Suck out cervix, its small knot of disease, four
suspicious signal lymph glands gallant in their defense,
organs of making drawn quick through the slick vaginal mouth
between legs splayed, restrained,
tied to the operating table soaked with blood.
What comes last? The useless appendix, faithful
observer of two miscarriages, collector of bits of skin,
hangnails chewed to the quick, indigestible
seed husks gnawed after unspeakable loss.
Gone, now, lying in surgical stainless steel pans.
Gone her mind a nova blown open
to particulate matter piercing sexless dimensions
of darkness as comforting and safe as stars she glides between.
She has left her body with its terrible scars.
What will she remember years from now as she sits at her morning table,
sipping her ration of caffeine, watching wild birds fight over seed?
The way she was gutted by strangers who scrubbed her abdomen
of any trace of woman. Her all-too human grief.
Still, she is alive.
Alive. Her scream celebrates the strength to make a fist,
to lift her head, rise
against the constant throb of absence.
The clock of making booms in her chest, asks
what kind of creature will she finally be?

SHAPESHIFTER

Each day I climb onto fear's broad shoulders, tape
my fingers to fragile reins, weaving them through
the unpredictable angry mane.

The future is a cracked ice cube
plunked in the imagination's teeming water glass.
Chemo's breath stinks, could take my life with no regrets.

Fear is a shapeshifter with bloody teeth
or no teeth at all, just a broken jaw of anxiety.
Holding tight to grief's violin, its arms bruise.
What ifs are its favorite cuisine.

No one can predict how fear can leap
up from a birthday cake or laugh like a monkey on fire.
Fear is a horse starving for grain.

Fear grinds down the raw ore of the heart,
smelting each nodule of grief, removing
its aggregate shield.

I have to make you sick to make you well,
        the oncologist says, *five months*
we'll scour each cell of your abdomen clean.

INTRAPERITONEAL CHEMO

Before each infusion, the recipe seems placid,
carefully weighed, seven and a half pounds
of fluid wrung from platinum, purest of all metals,
in a bag hung from the hook, liquid Book of the Dead
above my head. In the treatment room,
there is no art, just the stern tilt of the hospital bed,
a visitor's steel chair. Even the light is frugal.
I remember the scorpion bite dark as venous blood,
clear as the IV needle a nurse stabs
through the membrane of the port sewn
onto my lower rib to pour toxins into my emptied womb.
It always burns, multiplies thousands of bone splinters
stinging cells, murdering nerves, dulling
my mind, my spine alive, a drawn bow
aimed at heaven, sprouting agony's three stingy feathers.

GREEN FLAME

Slender as my ring finger, the female hummingbird crashed
into plate glass separating her and me
before we could ask each other's name. Green flame,
she launched from a dead eucalyptus limb.
Almost on impact, she was gone, her needle beak
opening twice to speak the abrupt language of her going,
taking in the day's rising heat as I took
one more scalding breath, horrified by death's velocity.
Too weak from chemo not to cry
for the passage of her emerald shine,
I lifted her weightlessness into my palm.
Mourning doves moaned, *who, who,*
oh who while her wings closed against the tiny body
sky would quick forget as soon as it would forget mine.

TOWARD WINGS

Between sleep and what assumes to be real, I pick up the old sword
cutting sutures from wounds sewn with the raw sinews of fear.
I remember flying from my horse atop the Kyber Pass,
my brother charging, heartbroken and fierce to avenge my death.
This time I pull the spear from my chest,
cauterize that terrible wound with burning feathers,
the hooked beak of the eagle buoyed by wind.

Dreams are a way out as much as a way in to the labyrinth.
Since surgery, dreams are black velvet fists curled
sleeping in sacred rooms. Sutured as those layered incisions
closing deep wounds, they refuse to open.

Where did they throw the tumors, my cancered womb,
cervix, fallopian tubes?
The ovaries that bloomed disease?

Fear grows like basil in a pot spun of anxiety and self-loathing.
Stop watering it with tears, and it dies.
No little violins play.
Little violins recall the scalpel. The trick
is not to listen to pity clinging to their strings.

A black-chinned hummingbird drops from the dead saguaro arm
to the pink-mouthed blossom for nectar, drinks
deep through its messenger beak.

Sun reaches through monsoon clouds, blades of light,
pulling me skyward, toward
wings I cannot see.

SONG OF REPRIEVE
for Reggie Arthur

Desert broom sweeps sky clean, sweeps
the orange songs of goldfinches and warblers
into its branches, hallelujahs of joy.
Feathers, too, are small brooms grooming air
we navigate to breathe.

I push aside pain, thin and screeching
like slices of mica under tires, my lessons
old as lizards whose ancestors slid
under the booming feet of brontosaurus
grazing the high branches of rainforest trees
that fire and memory morphed into this desert.

Pain redirects the arc of my arms and legs
in their simple intent of motion.
The suffering of lizards is as keen as my own.

ON LOSING A MOTHER

for Joy Harjo

Face west.
This is the doorway open for the leap.
You know the protocols, chants, food that loves her.

Bathe what shrinks, the disappearing length of her arms,
ankles, the feet each hour more lucent than the hour before.
Watch the ark of the chest as it fills with dusk,
the way breath must darken as it leaves.

You've driven hundreds of miles to find her
amid the stained sheets of childhood,
tangled in wool blankets and bedsores.
She smiles, wants biscuits and gravy for breakfast.
The morphine drips.

It is the same song repeating itself across the globe,
the way we circle one another like elephants
comforting a wounded sister or like water
that doubles back to eat its own corpse.

This is the body of the blood you feasted on
as a fetus orbiting inside her womb. You
are her singing in a winter kitchen
when love forgot the keys to the house,
her breath, her light,
her dark tears.

To say goodbye, stroke her hair gone to silver wire,
her bare arms. Listen,
even though she has lost her voice,

speaks now only with her eyes
that hold each trembling leaf of you.

Hold her hand, place
your heart over her heart
to absorb the dual cadence, a cappella devotional,
sheet music of the unsaid you've come to understand.

Who is your witness? Your sister and your brother
          hover over her bed. Her eyes open
the color of deep sea water seeping
into the *cenote* of your own wild places. Her eyes
          see beyond the shadows her children make.

Ready yourself for her leap.
It will surprise you no matter
how many times you've practiced in your head.
Leaving is like this, a wrenching away to peace.

Turn inside her as she turns
to the throbbing inside a ceremonial drum,
a song of honor for your mother
dying in all her perfect imperfections.

Air is filling her bones, turning them into birds,
into reed flutes, just as sure as her spirit fills the room
where you have prepared all of her favorite foods.

DHARMA
for Marnie Hillsley

Blue sky breathes through hummingbird's throat.
Who made the moat where red ants and Harris's Hawk dream?
My fingers lace clouds into a shawl
of thunder and wind. I think of a friend,
whose face I've never touched, how
to memorize all the colors of her eyes,
how ever to sing for her the way
eagle feathers catch the sure intent of stars.

Ah, to wake in the desert, creosote-heady with last night's rain,
breeze cool as glass fingering palo verde's
buttery blooms, a collared lizard
in iridescent armor creeping from the Spanish Bayonet, five
baby quails noodling to strewn seed.

I hold out for the calliope hummingbird
who mines orange trumpet flowers
reaching beyond itself
with its long black tongue.
We feed a long line of hungry ghosts.

Changing shape a thousand times a morning, clouds
never stop loving wind
pushing them over the horizon's brink.
The heart is memory's toughest muscle.
Break the mirror. Never forget
one lovely jagged piece.

WALKING THE LABYRINTH
for Melissa Pritchard

PERSEPHONE

I am not the first half life shifting
between the underworld
and what passes for birdsong
hidden by the drenched branches of evergreens.
Every two weeks, thin wires of platinum,
sap extracted from the yew tree
storms my blood, and I'm thrown
into Pluto's suffocating arms, dizzied,
seeking a cure, to heal time
spinning at the heart of disease.

IMPLOSION

A building becomes a vacuum, becomes
a woman who loses breath,
to rebuild herself, a few beams missing each time,
keeps the leaded glass doors to her heart
open, washes her windows, lemon juice
clean, flings them wide
to a gypsy mountain breeze.

FEED THE BIRDS

The Dalai Lama's astrologer admonished,
"When you feel very bad, when
you are suffering, feed the birds."

Each day I refill the feeder
for house finches, Gambel's quail,
the cloud-fearing mourning doves,
Say's phoebe, white-throated sparrows, the last
lingering winter hummingbirds
sipping nectar red as Kool-Aid or
the inner lips of bougainvillea
stunning the Thanksgiving porch.

THE WALL

In a photo, a man's hand slips
between huge welded metal plates
of the ignorant wall we built, separating
Mexico from our hearts, just ninety miles away.
His hand cups his wife's waist.
Solace doesn't recognize walls
that stop an embrace, split
families as if they're disposable
cords of balsa wood
to stoke xenophobia's hearthfire of fear.

FRANKENSTORM

In every convergence, separation shifts
what would ground us, what walls
might open our hearts. A storm,
converging hurricane, snowstorm, rain,

a tidal surge over a thousand miles wide
eats the Eastern shore.

Weeks after, searchers
uncover legions of the drowned.

In every convergence wings greet dawn and dusk, love
swirling through a crenulated brain that invents songs,
another kind of compassion we fail to emulate, the dance
tapped out from branch to wet branch we could learn
to lift us from the vast country of loneliness
fashioned from desire's dissatisfied threads.

FOOD VS FRACKING

Who sets Pluto's table
inside earth, mother
we've ravished and stolen from?
Even trees uproot themselves
trying to get our attention.
How much oil can we extract
from her breasts, how much methane

drawn up as toxic fire
from the underworld
through a piped web of destruction
beneath schoolyards where children run
with laughter they invent
as they invent the world each day?

THE GIFT OF THE LABYRINTH

Fingering the cool piano black rock walls, Persephone
breathes on his brow made of flames and death, sings

The way in is the way out. Who knows
which path leads
                    to her own monster's cave?

THEORIES OF TIME

What dimension lies beyond time?
—Alfred Corn

I imagine you writing by computer light blue as veins
under aging skin, the question a quark shooting from pale fingers
dodging invisible photons between stars orbiting their own dimensions.
Is time simply a light switch we flip on and off, defining a life?

In broken Vietnamese, Ahn says her daughter collapsed.
At seventeen she needs a new liver, her arteries nearly blocked,
her disease so rare it is shared by one in one million.
Ahn hired the ambulance to drive her a hundred miles to the Mayo Clinic,
where she waits on a transplant list. Her survival depends
on timing, the death of another she'll never know.

On NPR, a reporter interviews a survivor of the Brussels
subway bombing, the mad sparrows of fear flying blind
via satellite as she describes the carnage at rush hour, how
blood soaked her new sweater. She did not see the suicide bomber,
flew out of her body, didn't know whether the blood was hers or his.

Beyond time, memory shimmers like the scales of a diamondback
in desert sun. In what dimensions does the rattlesnake believe
as she strikes the kangaroo rat? What does the rat
remember of his childhood? The watch he never received?

A carpenter bee, big as my thumb, batters my window.
Behind him, the door is thrown wide to the sky.
I fetch a glass, trap his incessant buzz, cap it
with a health insurance bill, take him out
to fly over the thorns of a prickly pear.
He has no need for thanks or to glance back.

Every six months I drive to the Mayo Clinic for a CAT scan
and blood tests. Routine never stops biting its nails on anxiety.
In the lab, I strip, wait in a thin gown with other survivors
to check whether our cancer has recurred. I love them all.
It is a little like Russian roulette, each test marked by the turn of the barrel,
by the snap of metal on metal blowing out the known world.

I want to write you that your poetry always matters
no matter what dimension it sings to. If it can move me
thousands of miles away, it can move a photon in space.

I want to find a new healthy liver for Ahn's daughter
so she may dance beyond time. I want all of us
beyond time and heartbreak, shattering
the speed of light with our craft, our hearts unblocked,
flying from the glass jars of our fear,
to a dimension beyond thorns or the end of time.

OLIVIA BEGINS CHEMOTHERAPY
for Olivia Garza

Burnished copper pink, low clouds
bunch like sheep driven by dawn wildfire.
Friday and Olivia begins chemo, round one, taxol
derived from yew trees growing in a rainforest far
from the hot bottle fly buzz of Tucson.
Round one of four, she steps into the ring, wrists taped,
fists up to protect her face. Pathologist, Olivia knows
her chemistry, tags each dividing cell in her memory,
charts the spread of tumors loading her ovaries,
knows cancer's terrible speed as it leaps
organ by organ, attaches to feed like mushrooms
in a warm damp basement unseen.
Olivia knows her science, learns
now the hammer of pain,
neuropathy stealing her feet.
In amped desert heat, her cats
craze each day, leaping from scratching pad
to couch to chair to counter, bounding
across Saltillo floors looking for her to play.
Their meows rattle double-paned windows
as the sun sears through palo verde, mesquite.
Chemo nurses are always kind.
When the needle pops through her port, Olivia
closes her eyes, pulls tight the prayer shawl
against the hospital chill, feels saline flush her veins,
In med school, she learned the names of drugs
and their uses—comfort of antacid, steroid hype cancelled
by Benadryl fog. Then taxol's slow burn,

scouring.

Scouring.

Scouring.

Ignoring fear's clawsy, Olivia leans full into the pain.

SOLAR ECLIPSE IN THE LAND OF
SANDSTONE HOODOOS AND CRANES

Between hoodoos and the ghosts of whooping cranes,
day dies too soon. Secure against Siberian ice, my ancestors
sing against the sorrow of light vanishing.

The white wolf flops under a rabbit bush, moans
at the kingbird flying low to catch gnats and blow flies.
Long shadows take us in their hollow mouths.

We listen to sky's intelligence, wait for the shift
from glare to humble shade. In my pocket jiggle stones—
one carnelian, one black jet the shape of a falcon's eye.

Gemini moon blocks the Gemini sun—twins canceling twins.
What can that mean for me, small Gemini woman hunched
in the penumbra of balancing rocks stranded in a dry Ice Age sea?

My rescue dog circles like my fears to curl on the slim ledge
where I perch near rocks reaching for the dark
astrologers predict will change everything.

Unafraid, my love climbs the crumbling spine of the ridge, aims
his lens at the exact path the eclipse takes over our heads.
In this way, his Mediterranean tribe survived for centuries.

We are as forgotten as this gulch, as stunted as jojoba and
desert broom who give up their burden baskets of heat
to the dark cauldron sky has become.

FINDING A MOTH DEAD ON THE WINDOWSILL
for John Uschuk, d. 2010

Astonishing this cecropia, the color of juniper bark,
its thin wings thrust back as if it dove through the stars
just to die here. What broke its flight
while night froze around its intent? I wait a breath
before I touch its final beauty, wonder
if my brother's broad chest thrust up
to expel the moth wing of his last breath
in the veteran's hospice, where Agent Orange
could no longer scar his hands, where
napalm could not scald the scalps of children
he watched incinerating all his life, so that
orphanages called him in dreams, so that he
could not bear the slap of moth wings on his porch
beating insistent as the blades of the helicopter
he shared with body bags going home.

SINGING BOWL

Between human skull and blue handblown vase
sprayed with a glaze of stars, the singing bowl
calms incisions screaming arias
off-key after sugery to remove every
fecund organ in my belly.

    Its ringing could be Saturn's
hollow howl across black space
or the sound waves make underwater
as they moan the length of a blue whale's throat
calling for a mate she may never see.

What woman can hear the hissing register of stars,
watery echoes a mountain lion hears stalking
a wounded deer near dawn?

Do all orbs vibrate the third eye
as it wakes the forehead
to throb back to another life where,
a sailor, tying down the mainsail on a slave vessel,
is tossed quick as a sodden hanky into
the electric appetite of waves?

I hold the perfect solitude of hammered silver
in my hands, noticing just
over its metal rim a calliope hummingbird
sipping invisible waves from an empty feeder.

What song can grow new birth organs
from the disease the surgeon cut
from my riddled gut?

Each challenge is opportunity! The optimist exults,
opens palms to a storm. Lightning
scars my lips, singes words that would hum
as harmonic as light taking the trees.

I strike the bowl to divine its shadow song,
comforting vowels, long drawn, pity shorn.

SPEAKING OF ANGELS AND GHOSTS

WESTERN TANAGER

for Fenton Johnson

Back from hiking the far mountains, I find
your desiccated body perfect, black wings
tucked under the slick yellow back,
orange head intact but for eyes eaten by sky.

Slim sarcophagus you bear no wounds.
Neither owl, cat, or hawk tried to eat you.
Your petrified beak cocks its last song
to the invisible sea beyond Sombero Peak. Sleek,
your mummified carcass offers no clues.
Were you smashed to earth by monsoon or
did our picture window lure you to secure
branches growing in glass?

Beauty, I can't bury you, won't disturb your solemn rest
on the picnic table among presidential lies
in the New York Times, bellowing his urgent need
to build a twenty-foot-high steel wall to secure our border
from unarmed refugees. You nestle with turret shells
from the Sea of Cortez, a sand dollar said to
contain the crucifixion, lovely beyond belief.

Lithe acrobat
                too rarely have I seen you flip
through memory's eucalyptus leaves.
            Where do you sing?
                        A full moon collapses
like the Halloween pumpkins on the porch.
            I gentle you weightless to my shelf.
Time never rests,

its ghost prints leading us over a horizon giddy

with insistent light

we cannot conceive will ever end.

MORNING COFFEE

In my mug the ghosts of berries,
cut shine of rubies handpicked
inside burlap bags rocking on burros
upslope in Colombia, berries grown on trees
speaking the old language of clouds and poverty, seized
each afternoon by the hands of rain,
and shaken like children from dreams.

It starts here while the toucan sleeps
in rain forest squeezed by ocean and Andes.
Coffee is the eye of Cortez widening to burn herons
and flamingos in Aztec aviaries, coffee
the hand of Quetzalcoatl trembling as he lifts
a smoking mirror to see the blond giant, murdering.

Coffee does not run light as a gecko
across the tongue so much as curl between teeth,
waking me to a neighborhood of sirens
and domestic screams, to the sheet music of a mother's laughter
plaiting her daughter's hair, to the insults
of politicians on TV hydroplaning like car tires in a torrent,
to my fingertips drenched in caffeine
tapping like centipedes stampeding my kitchen table
under which the sleeping dog of reason breathes.

WEATHER CHANGE
for Terri Harvey

Wind slithers through oleander leaves like schools of salmon ghosts,
the iced relics of steelhead fins or silver lining rainbow trout cheeks

I held long ago as a girl. Sky chills even hidden scars.
The voices of desert birds are far away water trickling over a granite ledge.

Call out the colors of clean air, sweet, filling
the cancered lungs of my brother in the last veteran's hospice bed.

Call clean air for the lungs of women in Damascus or Kabul
who secretly perm the hair of other women in their homes

while husbands cloister, click beads, tongues lashing from tight mouths,
ignoring the slight breeze of words lilted by wives smothered

by centuries of swaddling cloth, by the slavery and comfort of veils.
Call sweet air. Fresh air for the mother bent into worry's hook,

air for the premature baby whose moth-wing lungs
struggle for flight in a neonatal unit across town,

air for the homeless man wandering paved drives
in our foothills community still asleep, his shoulders

drenched by a daypack so grimy its history is the cruelty of char.
Air for the pit bull snoring in a treeless gravel yard, chained

to a stake broiling in desert sun while his teen owner, a new
father, bags meth in his mother's bathroom.

Air for a child's hands closing on the first baseball of her life,
for the proton in the eye of the observer that changes

what a woman sees as love halfway across the globe.
Air for all of us, breathing memory's luminous mind,

the way quietly it says goodbye
from a river we will wade long after we say goodbye.

REFUGE

for Terry Acevedo

Since January, sun can't stop shivering.
Hope shakes her head, refuses to step inside the front door,
so we drive to San Xavier Mission smudged with mesquite smoke,
the thousand melted roses of perfumed candle wax.

Worn out, we retreat from paranoid tweets,
the confused sleight of hand from the Commander-in-Chief.
Who knows how many Russian pockets the President has lined?
Incarcerating migrant children along the border is the strategy of lies.

Under white bell towers, time reverses its hungry grind
patted by the hands of O'odham women stretching dough
to drop on hot tops of burn barrels, attended by dogs
and children's laughter as soft as sand they walk.

We enter the cathedral eyed by red archangels as we dip fingers
in bowls of holy water, our urgent need to cool nerves scraped raw
by the cries of children and toddlers ripped by federal agents
from parents seeking asylum in our country that's lost its heart.

The thousand flames of votives offer no solution
near San Francisco's effigy serene under blue satin.
It's said he grants miracles to those who lift his sacred head.
Since the election, mass on the reservation is packed.

Entering San Diego Capilla, we enter our own wounds, say
intentions for the dead, for the health of friends, for love to end
public lies so loud we've become deaf to every crisis cry.
We inhale the multiplicity of candle flames til our chests burst.

We stroll across the burning scalp of desert sun
to ramadas fashioned from ocotillo and ironwood trunks
to buy fry bread crisp with grease, tortillas
so thin you can see your fingers waving on the other side.

On unshaded railroad ties, we sit with families
breathing the sweet tincture of mesquite smoke, watch
a girl's head lean on her grandma's T-shirt sleeve, resting
away from alternative facts beating truth blind.

BORDERING ON HYSTERIA

I could border on hysteria, sew jaguars to the hem of my skirt, run
into traffic streaming north, hold out a sugar skull
to the president with hair the color of a dry wheat field that feeds no one.
But this poem doesn't have anything to do with comb-overs
or glacier eyes or gray suits signing laws a jaguar wouldn't stop to sniff
if they were smeared with rabbit blood and dropped in her path.

For the Tohono O'odham daughter roasting red chilis
over a mesquite fire to take to her diabetic father two houses away,
what is a border but a wall slung between
her kitchen table and his? For the screaming refugee babies jailed
in a "tender age" concentration camp near Brownsville?

This poem borders on anger knowing it will be
arrested for leaving water in the desert for families
fleeing with their shadows from the shadow puppet of poverty,
from genocidal armies, from ICE stealing their kids,
from the hands of coyotes ripping skirts off mothers
and daughters in van after van.

Poetry shouts, beating her fists raw against twenty-foot-high
steel plates dividing the heart of the nation, against
the magazines militia snap into semiautomatic rifles of rage
chasing a fourteen-year-old boy from Oaxaca through cactus
thorns that puncture our own skin.

I will not border on hysteria but will work
on a poem to feed all of us, a poem ground
from maize and jugs of fresh water to leave on the altar of need,
a poem with warm pillows and blankets to melt icy lies,

a poem to rock babies back to their mothers' arms,
a poem that erases the signatures of legislators
written by pens clenched in orange spray-tanned fists.

WEB

For months the web persists, one staunch string
tying the dead cholla arm to the living dipladenia vine,
hanging from it the intricate design, made by
a black widow and unfurling green tendrils
slow bottle flies land on to lay eggs
the spider wraps in silk.

I watch the tiny mummies multiply
guarded by the arachnid who glares at me.
I wonder whether vine and spider despise
or love one another.
Is their relationship simple necessity, a union
sealed with the wax of cooperation
bypassing emotion or desire?

How like a long marriage or friendship
taken for granted until the smash of wind's violent intent,
the mindless sweep of a broom.

This morning the web dangles,
spider's vanished with her red violin,
leaving a few fly mummies behind.
What gleams is that slim arm of a vine
stretching to the doorknob, dexterous
and as beautiful as calligraphy suspended
between the living and the dead who've moved on.

THE MORNING PORCH

for Don and Lynn Watt

We stumble though an upswept hairdo of morning song—
grackles whoop and clatter like broken ceramics
frothed by runoff spinning through a culvert
while the golden nape of a woodpecker soft-strokes the live oak
on its rollercoaster flap to the waterfall.
Legions of white-winged doves ask their singular
                              who oh who who who
to the socked-in pantheist sky.

Fog-beguiled illiterates overwhelmed by the half-recalled
paragraphs of half dreams, we speak in whispers
as if too much laughter this early might shatter the expanding universe,
our impossible need for clarity
to decode our own forgotten Rosetta stones.
Stunned as any clobbered frog by our hard rebirths
and blurred inside our shapeless desire,
we are so dumb with loneliness
we cannot really speak for wings we only guess.

Love is in the coffee steam, sharing cream
and the indecipherable chittering of squirrels
before fog banks shrink to reveal the all too real sweating sun.
Oh, this heavy San Antonio air is raw gray silk
that disguises each of us and our hunger
for bowls of fruit, their sticky pools of mingled juice,
the sweet grit of morning muffins.

What is art, but these fog-bound mornings
when we stagger from solitary sleep, learning
to bank the way a flock of swallows turn

all at once to feast on mosquitos,
scruffy feathers synchronized to a single reflective wing.

SPEAKING OF ANGELS AND GHOSTS

for Val Uschuk

My sister erects concrete angels to guard her house, angels
with small icy wings and full breasts, faces fierce
as Siberian wind that scoured our grandmothers,
angels androgynous, ghost white as borax, giant warriors
preserving tranquility in the old mining town where she creates.

My sister doesn't believe in ghosts, kicks superstitions in the teeth, even
though her intuition is honed sharp on a fine grindstone passed down
from our Grandma Anna's genes. She doesn't believe
in the blustering of a tyrant who lays down the law,
doesn't believe in men explaining the universe.
She sculpts beyond what she can see.

Agnostic, my father did not believe in churches or priests
holding out collection plates, but he believed in God, saw
the ghosts of buddies long dead laughing on his porch
under the vast black tidal night when everyone else was asleep.
They waved for him to join their wild party.
He told no one about this but me.

My mother's ghosts chased her through the web
of her mind's shifting gardens.
She howled with the invisible girl in her bedroom, made
stone circles in the moonlight of her agony.
Her ghosts buzzed like bottle flies terrifying
the windowsills of lonely. In the psyche hospital, she
spoke prophecies divined from desert trees in a voice far beyond me.

Guarding our front window a wooden angel holds her hands to her cheeks,
Her mouth the O in discovery, carved back turned

to gardenia's lounging sexual perfume.
I admire the vast intelligence of birds, animals, flowers, and trees, the way
wind sculpts sandstone, water
that absorbs light from clouds, earth's angels,
hands thrust elbow deep in lithe ghosts, articulate, alive.

ONE TO COUNT CADENCE

for Steve Ramirez

Before coffee, a Cooper's hawk soughs in, razor the feeder to scatter dawn birds.
Sun lifts machetes of light over the Rincons slicing through oleanders,
eucalyptus trees hanging breezeless in hammocks of dreams.

I email you those I see. Gila woodpecker teaches us to laugh
as it surfs shadows, pierces rush hour that roars up Oracle Road. Hammering
a palo verde trunk, this Gila tattoos runes for the future to read.

Anna's hummingbird drops through palo verde branches, joined
by its mate stitching air between green thorns. Smeared red on heads
and chests, house finch warriors fight sparrows for millet and black thistle seed.

I could hold them all in my hands. We understand the word flutter
as onomatopoeia, wings chittering from feeder to feeder
above Gambel's quail who waddle in from the wash

they've shared all night with the snuffling quarrels of javelina,
with coyote screams and the spilled blood of desert hares quivering.
Each morning, we trade bird counts, the only news worth hearing.

It's too early to learn how many children Assad choked
with Sarin gas, how many Tomahawk missiles hissed back
to make our leader, who bought his way out of boot camp, a war hero,

too early to predict how many migrant children and toddlers will fry
paid for by our tax money or how the blowhard preens, snaps on his gold Rolex, knots
his $15K tie while parents instruct their children how to eat vouchers for lunch.

From my porch, I can see the mountain smolder from last night's human-lit fire.
    The mountain hunkers in smoky haze, like a mourning dove
        when the Cooper's hawk dives in for a kill on its evitable wings.

HOLOGRAMS

for Patricia Spears Jones

This is desert's finest season, season of California poppies
sunset yellow and holding up cups of blood-orange light
next to penstemon's Elizabeth Taylor lipstick blooms, translucent
waxy pink aloe, stunted lupine singing the blues,
greasewood's yellow flowers verdins consume,
month of mating butterflies and white-winged doves, month
of new desert hares and bobcat kits mewling in our neighbor's eaves, month before
heat's warriors run amok and fires eat the trees, month of Syrian
mothers wiping blood from their babies' mouths, month of political screams
giving birth to semi-automatic fists, threats of hunger worldwide, melting ice caps,
month of coal-fired power plants doubling sulfuric smoke, while we survive
hallucinatory as the future etched on a computer screen.

AFTER THE ELECTION, THE SUPER MOON RISES
OVER THE RINCON MOUNTAINS

The mountains are burning and we cannot sleep.

We light candles at the Grotto where daughters toss the dark braids of sick mothers
at Guadalupe's feet, where fathers pin photos of the stricken for slivers of miracle,
uphill from the Mission's dome, White Dove catching sunset's bioluminescent votes.

We inhale the dust of conquistadors who must applaud these election results
caught in the tyrant's clenched teeth despising the cracked sidewalks of the poor
who believe his promises thin as shadows disappearing at their feet.

The mountains are burning out of control, flames higher than our dreams of peace,
eating pine trees, the hearts of deer, flames higher than grand hopes
or any despot's fiery rhetoric of lies.

At hill crest, we sit on concrete losing heat to stark dark taking desert
in its irrevocable mouth, sit stunned despite the stinging bites
of the fire ant colony skittering up our invading calves.

Unsheltered, we cannot sleep, see the huge yellow corona crown,
the birth of our moon closer to earth than it's been since our own
entrances to this world more than half a century past.

We wait, holding tight our arms against news that darkens daily, against
the crisp flap of white sheets, the sneering narcissist chorus recounting rapes on TV.
There is nothing else to do but lean into one another's sorrow, our disbelief.

We've left candles of hope burning in the maw of the Grotto below
to witness the balm of moon rise while mountain slopes turn inferno
sending contrails of smoke to choke twilight's last blue song.

Oh, Moon, you are so late, grinding up slow behind jagged Rincon peaks, backlit
carrying enough gleaming milk to feed thousands of refugee children hunted by
border guards. Have you heard their small bones cry sleepless in detention cells?

We watch wildfires immense as our nightmares consume miles of ridges,
burning past our history. Corona of ice, the invisible moon
blesses supplicant cacti offering thorns to heaven.

Closer we shiver until a blizzard of crushed diamonds breaks white,
striking us blind, cauterizing our battered hearts, rejecting the nuclear
wasps of power and revenge hissing from the tyrant's tongue.

Moon's perfect snow glows sharp as an arctic blade slicing open arms, baptizing
our faces with reflected light. Gandhi was right. All tyrants must fall.
Under her scrutiny, no gold-plated dynasty can last.

Moon's icy chin lifts for Venus. Mica glitters each step over volcanic rock past
the Grotto's knotted prayers for compassion, past long burning candles, navigating
treacherous gravel the color of winter fields, taking us home, beyond any terror or grief.

LET THEM EAT CAKE

Trumpet vines die in winter. Rio Dipladenia's delicate tendrils lift blood-colored
petals hummingbirds thrust beaks into sucking up nectar. Reaching for sun, vines
yearn for heat, remember which leaves frost took first. The heart is the body's toughest
muscle. It is the exact color of dipladenia blooms.

In Florida, manatees stuff hyacinths into their huge soft mouths, have not read
the book of beauty and myth as human. My brother died in Florida, lush peninsula
mapped by long-legged birds, waterways choked by water lilies and pet boa
constrictors released, Florida sparkling with oil-slicked Gulf coquinas flipped by
surf onto white sand. War veteran drenched by Agent Orange, my brother choked on
food, his esophagus, frail lace, cancer ate from his stomach to his throat.

The President describes chocolate layer cake so rich it drenched his gold-rimmed
plate as he cut deals with the Japanese Prime Minister above the Caribbean's turquoise
bay at Mar-A-Lago cleared of manatees, beaches raked pristine, lifeless. The President
twists his gold wrist watch, signs an executive order to open up off-shore drilling
far from his turreted resort, scowls as he holds up the edict on TV.

Trumpet vines can grow five inches overnight, flowers opening to birds, the least
shiver of wind, their hearts beating faster than fingers typing a love poem. Flowers are
seldom alone, see in the dark, grow in sun and moon light. My brother did not like cut
flowers, said like all beauties, they only died.

Swimming a cataract deep in a crystal stream, manatee bumped my diver brother,
mouthed his beard while he hovered weightless under the surface. When she hugged
him, he thought he'd drown. He said he wouldn't have minded dying that way, tangled
in hyacinths, smothered by a mermaid's embrace.

TV news prattles through the living room I avoid, close focused on our president's
golf game. He tees off, duffs a chunk of earth from beneath his feet, tweets

the game was rigged, the camera full of lies, shakes his small fists,
threatening to build a higher wall.

Hummingbirds don't lie, tongues quick as flame deconstructing nectar in their gullets.
On PBS news flashes the photo of thirty-seven-year-old Sergeant Garcia, no story,
only that he died in Afghanistan. There is no Hummer tire he knelt beside, pinned
by Taliban fire. No taste of phosphorus, choking the birds. Just Sergeant Garcia fading.

Trumpet vines do not watch TV, thriving in desert heat in porch shade. Serenaded
by cactus wrens, yellow-headed verdins, they sing in the language of green. We never
cut off their blooms. My brother's cancer multiplied to his adrenals, liver and lungs.
His heart was the last organ to die.

GOOD FRIDAY AT OLD PASCUA

Deer dancer ties on moth cocoons to his calves, ties on antlers, swirls rattles
filled with seeds while the Yaqui Marias in flowing gowns glow white as the moon
far from the blonde destroyer who pins on a fourteen-karat gold American flag
to his Armani lapel, calls out his military to bomb a desert halfway across the globe.
I pull on boots, sweater, my best jeans. I'd walk on my knees to enter the flower world.
Good Friday and in Old Pascua the procession continues, *chapayekas*
waving hand painted wood swords at black-coated *fareseos*, telling the old story
of good chasing evil from the world. For weeks, the whole village dances days and
nights, stamping love's renewal through the soles of sandaled feet to rhythms
old as moonlight deer nibble in ocotillo, old as betrayal cracking the lips of Judas, old
as the fifteen pieces of silver burning his hands, rhythms old as dictators who
believe they are saviors, who smash the vulnerable who pray for peace.
Deer dancer tilts his head, lifts a foot to the grind of raspados. His heart taps to the
waterdrum's beat, to the *shush, shush, shush* of cocoons. Tonight, deer antlers point
our way through terrible thorns of sacrifice to hope's lush and edible blooms.

CONTEMPLATING FIRE ON A SPRING DESERT EVENING

My dog and I contemplate fire after hiking the dry arroyo,
striding past pencil cactus, mesquite bold with new leaves, small
bouquets of fuchsia wildflowers, coachwhip lizards springing from our feet
disturbing their sleep. It's been years since
I made a fire in this hearth, listened to the way fire speaks,
flapping its velvet tongues, its squealing and insistent
banter before it settles into radiance.
We could be outside courting coyotes screeching
after hares in the wash while desert willows
and creosote cool night's fine silk skin. Or
we could watch Rachel Maddow skewer the President
whose budget cuts breakfast for the children of the hungry
who voted his promises in, supported by Congress lockjawed along Party lines.
We take notes from what burns, the long patience of ironwood,
spiking heat engendered from its dense flesh, the way a few logs last
for hours unlike the brash flash and pop of ponderosa pine
or the quick self-immolation of birch. How many centuries
we've sat around fires, keeping stories, making
songs, our history woven in ash. We are all part of a story
scarred by fires we create. While our nation
screams from war to war, from one hatred to another,
we contemplate fire piercing the oncoming dark.

NO APRIL FOOLS

From the faded patio umbrella, a protective mask
basks in sunrise, dangling like a parachute
or tanager nest catching the early breeze
that stirs eucalyptus leaves. If we get COVID-19
we can steam them to draw our last breath.
Across town rush hour is hushed, the crush of diesel
exhaust tamping the city of risk. Worry sinks
infected claws in our dreams. Every
sneeze or cough is suspect. Through
the picture window, Sadie Cat
stares at birds whirring to dwindling seed.
Mourning doves eat from St. Francis's bowl
while sweet finches and sparrows flock
to feeders hung from palo verde limbs.
This season of wildflowers and cactus buds
brings little relief from news that 200,000
of us will soon die. It's a conservative estimate.
Words won't form themselves but swirl
like fear's bleach scouring away the American Dream
too fast to translate the fatal language of its burn.

LEVITATION

Each night the owl of sorrow undresses her
as she pretends to fly from his hands.
How many of us have mistaken Venus
for Jupiter with all its nattering moons
strung like uncut opals along its equator?
How many of us have believed the lie?
There are men whose tongues cut
syllables into stilettos
from the unfurling human cloth of kindness, men
who would build the wall higher
and thicker between countries, who would plant
surveillance cameras in their wives' camisoles.
She can find no nightgown of mercy in her dim closet,
no constellation of hope growing like quartz crystals
in a cool glass of water in her mother's kitchen.
She wants to lick her own fingers, pull
them like plows down her lover's cheeks,
but they've run off with the owl to count stars
in the bottom of someone else's cup
from which she refuses to drink.

DESERT AUBADE

Months now the rare jaguarundi has not crossed
evening's path to the arroyo splitting our neighborhood.
We miss its fluid mahogany leap between ocotillo
and creosote, the way it snaps the landscape alive
then disappears complete, proving, indeed,
you can never twice step into the same stream.

Each morning, we resist news reports dropping
like cyanide into coffee, wait til after breakfast to digest
new atrocities stripping every humanitarian bone
from the exquisite corpse of our national conscience.

Before dawn, the dogs bolt from the kitchen door,
scatter finches, cactus wrens, desert hares
they can't begin to catch in their snapping jaws.
Relentless sun rises in its catacomb of light.
The coffee maker quarrels with leftover crumbs
on the counter while the homeless begin to wake
in the bottom of the wash behind our house.

We are just as culpable as the White House, looking
away from the disheveled man sunburned to char and
jerking in his bones as he walks the berm of rush hour
on Oracle Road, looking instead for the jaguarundi's return,
avoiding thorns turned by sunrise the color of our common blood.

THE ESSENTIAL SHAPE
for Clarence Cruz

Spinning, the earth begins, shapes itself with fingers of light.
We spin on the hub of Pueblo sun rising
inside clay dug from earth's wound repaired by medicine songs,
prayers of forgiveness. Earth carries us, heals
our wounds as we spin on the hub of desire.

Buddhists say kill all desire. Fire
burns the same in any language, births what we create.

Turtle rises on clawed clay feet luminescent
as the wheel of night stars. The potter's sacred pattern
incises clay the way a tattooist scars skin to protect it,
the design immortal in a mortal world.

Slap. Slap. On the studio shelf the master shape,
crenulated mouth open to wind song, bowl
holding constellations of eternity in its wet body
the kiln chooses to harden or explode.

Slap. Slap. There is no unbreakable form.
What spins flies apart or adheres like the supreme
idea of water pouring through the Milky Way.

Somewhere the ghosts of my people knead clay
dug from a river bed in spring, clay black
as the iris of an owl eye at midnight,
black as the bruised mouths of rifle barrels
in the hands of Bolsheviks who will murder them.
Fire will burn down their house.

I hear my Belarus grandmothers scream
down the stars, memories of bullets shattering waistcoats,
the simplest dresses in their long ago house
burned to the revolutionary ground that ran red
far from the teeth of these red cliffs.

Slap. Slap. A student fashions Matryoshka dolls
so real, they startle me, far from home.

Thousands of miles gone. There is only connection.

Each glittering doll nestles in the other's heart.
Not one doll is empty, is guardian and refugee,
individual as the fingerprints of a potter
pulling the essential shape from earth's wounds.

GARDENIAS AT EASTER

On a January morning after World War II, my mother carried gardenias
as she walked the aisle in the small stone Michigan chapel where my lovestruck father
waited, towering over everyone in her life, including her parents who warned against
a wild Russian immigrant soaked in blood from battles that distanced his blue eyes.

Forty years later, I carried gardenias at my own wedding to the dark gypsy poet
I could not live without, my longing a silk canoe that carried me underground,
between swampy impenetrable trees to the orgasmic sea. Gardenias scented my arms,
my breasts, gardenias flame white as Ahkmatova's nights outside the Lubyanka

where her husband was shot, her son starved for writing individual ideas.
It was the one sure way to murder the poet, Stalin must have believed.
To the altar, I carried gardenias the way I carried my desire, pressed into my chest,
their visceral musk becoming my skin, heady as dark chocolate–smeared lips.

On the early porch, eight gardenias take the air we breathe. We turn off news of war's
imminent jaws. Desert flowers have never seemed so lush, tongue red penstemon,
blue star flowers, the buttery pouts of California poppies cancelling out nuclear
weapons, our armada steaming for Syria, Korea, China, all points East.

Easter, and we are drunk on gardenias that resurrect us, that call us back

ecstatic to the forgotten silk chambers of our desire.